CONTENTS

KU-204-603

Colour affects us all, we are surrounded by it during the day in our workspaces and in our homes, it affects our conscious and, subliminally, our unconscious mind. A simple change to a colour scheme can completely change the mood of a room so evoking a totally new atmosphere. Colour is the most important factor when deciding to redecorate your home and careful consideration needs to be given to the effect you want to create.

The purpose of this book is to inspire you to experiment with some of the varied colours that are available from the ready-to-use paint ranges. All the colours used in this book, with the occasional exception, are from the ready-to-use, rather than specially mixed, ranges of paint and show just how easy it is to create stunning paint effects without needing to use specialist materials and finishes.

The theme of this book has been influenced by different countries throughout the world. With each chapter we are taken through a world of colour, from the rich and vibrant colours of India to the cool, calm sophistication of Scandinavia. Each chapter offers you a host of ideas to fire the imagination together with helpful practical advice and tips to bring the looks to life.

Different paint techniques are explored to create the various looks using step-by-step photographs. For example, in the Indian living room we use a naive form of decoration which involves a simple dot technique using only the forefinger, and in the Scandinavian set you can see how to construct intricate, leafy wall panelling. The step-by-step instructions are easy to follow and the hints and tips boxes will anticipate and solve any problems that might occur.

Stencilling, colour rubbing, sponging, colour washing and splattering are just some of the special paint effects that we help you to perfect. New, stylish looks can be achieved throughout the home and a buyer's guide at the end of the book will ensure you buy the right kind of paint and have everything to hand before you begin.

3 0012 00211498 0

COLLINS
HOME GUIDE

PAINTING
IDEAS

WITHDRAWN FROM STOCK

G-88 453
645
2

LIMERICK COUNTY LIBRARY

BY LINDA BARKER
PHOTOGRAPHY BY LIZZIE ORME

HarperCollinsPublishers

This edition published 1997 by
HarperCollins*Publishers*

Text © ICI Paints 1994

The text and illustrations in this book were previously
published in 1994 in *Dulux World of Colour* by Linda Barker
with project coordination by Welbeck Golin/Harris Communication Limited

A catalogue for this book is available from the British Library

Linda Barker
is an interior designer and author specializing in the art of paint techniques.

Lizzie Orme
is a photographer working in the field of interior design whose work is
regularly seen in books and national magazines.

All rights reserved

ISBN 0 00 413 003 0

Printed and bound in Hong Kong

NEW PLASTER

● This must be dry. Holes and cracks should be filled with a suitable filler, allowed to dry and then rubbed down smooth with glasspaper.

● Before painting, dust the wall with an old, clean, dry paint brush to remove all debris.

● Emulsion paint can then be applied direct to the clean, prepared surface. Vinyl matt finish is the best choice for new, bare plastered walls, as this allows any moisture left in the plaster to escape. The first coat should be thinned with tap water by up to 20 per cent. This will make it much easier to apply and will ensure good adhesion of the paint to the surface.

PREVIOUSLY PAINTED WALLS

● It is always a good idea to clean the entire area with soapy water first. This will remove any grime or grease which could prevent the paint from drying. It is important to rinse with clean water afterwards. Loose, flaking or chipped areas must be scraped away and then sanded smooth. Fill any cracks and other imperfections with an interior plaster filler. When dry rub down smooth and dust off.

● Where the surface has been painted with a solvent-based paint, e.g. a gloss paint, normal emulsion paints will not adhere particularly well to the surface. Specialist kitchen and bathroom paints will adhere to the surface, provided that it is thoroughly abraded with glasspaper first to gain a matt appearance. Brush with an old paint brush to remove any dust.

DECORATING PAPERED WALLS

● Stripping wallpaper is both time-consuming and extremely boring as well as very hard work, particularly if it has been painted. A steam stripper will make the job much easier. These can be hired from a local hire shop. If the paper is in good condition it can be painted over again as long as it is firmly stuck down and the wall is sound.

● The main problem with painting over patterned or coloured wallpaper is one of bleeding or staining of parts of the pattern through the paint. Use a tester pot of paint first to test this, allowing the paint to dry overnight before buying a bigger can if all is well. If staining does occur, the safest solution is the complete removal of the wallpaper.

● Not all wallpapers are suitable for painting. Vinyl-coated or washable wallpapers must always be removed first.

● If the wallpaper is to be completely stripped, then ensure that all paste residue from the wallpaper is also removed from the surface. To do this, use plenty of warm water, a wallpaper stripping knife and a clean sponge. It is easy to tell if paste residues remain as the surface will feel rough to the touch. Alternatively, line the walls with lining paper first, in which case such thorough preparation will not be required.

HINTS AND TIPS

● Read all the instructions on the back of the paint can thoroughly **before** you start to paint.

● Wear eye protection when preparing surfaces and when painting.

● Wear gloves to protect sensitive hands. If you do get paint on your skin, do not clean it off with white spirit but wash immediately with a proprietary skin cleaner or soap and water.

● Make sure you remove any wax polish from the paintwork – it often collects on the skirtings next to polished floors. Failure to do so will impair the adhesion and drying of the paint.

PREPARING PAINTED WOODWORK

● Clean the paintwork to remove all dirt, oil, grease and other contamination. Wash the paintwork with a solution of warm soapy water or sugar soap. Pay particular attention to the areas around door handles and window catches, where dirt and grease will be heaviest, then rinse with fresh water. It is important to change the rinsing water regularly.

● Remove all loose and defective paint by scraping with a paint scraper, then thoroughly rub down with glass paper and dust off. Alternatively, for a really smooth surface on gloss-painted surfaces, use fine grade wet-and-dry abrasive paper dipped in water. This will give a very smooth, matt finish.

● Any bare patches of wood need to be primed with a suitable wood primer first. Then build up the resultant low spots gradually with undercoat, lightly sanding between coats when dry. Then apply an undercoat to the whole surface, followed by the gloss paint. The same process can be used when applying other finishes, such as satinwood with Teflon, using a first coat of satinwood instead of undercoat. This will help to blend in the areas where all the old paint has come off.

● If you live in an older property, especially in a pre-1960 building, the wood and metal surfaces may have been painted with paint made with lead pigments. Special care must be taken when sanding or stripping. A simple leaflet explaining how it should be removed safely is available free of charge from the ICI Paints Advice Centre, Wexham Road, Slough SL2 5DS.

BRUSHES FOR THE JOB

● For the best results always use good quality brushes. The quality of the brush used has a direct effect upon the quality of the finished job and the ease with which the paint is controlled and applied.

● A good brush is carefully shaped towards a taper or wedge shape and has a good length of bristle. This holds the paint well and helps to apply it where you want it.

● Cheap brushes have short, stubby bristles and are usually 'wedged' with a piece of wood in the middle. A pure bristle brush is always the best choice. A good quality brush will get better with age, as it gets 'broken in'.

● When applying the new generation of water-based paints (e.g. water-based gloss or satinwood), a nylon polyester brush will give the best results. A bristle brush will tend to swell and distort as it absorbs the water in the paint, whereas nylon does not hold the water.

● Before putting a new brush into the paint, flick the bristles backwards and forwards a few times – this helps to get rid of dust and loose bristles.

BRUSH SIZES

● For most walls and ceilings use a 10cm (4in) or 12cm (5in) brush. For smaller areas such as coving, it is more practical to use 2.5–5cm (1–2in) brushes.

● When painting doors with any solvent-based paint, use 5–7.5cm (2–3in) brushes.

● Use a 5–7.5cm (2–3in) size brush for 'cutting in' around the tops of walls, edges of ceilings, skirtings etc. Use a 2.5cm (1in) brush or special angled brush for 'cutting in' window frames.

HINTS AND TIPS

● Avoid wearing woollens or other clothes which could shed fluff onto paintwork.

● Try to complete a whole area (wall, door etc.) at one time, or you will leave marks where the paint has dried.

● Ensure that rooms are properly ventilated: open windows and doors during both application and drying.

● Allow solvent-based paints, such as gloss, several days to harden before putting items back on shelves.

● Clear the room as completely as possible. Any items too big to remove should be stacked in the middle of the room and covered. Protect carpeting if it cannot be lifted. Be especially careful when using thinned paint as it is more likely to drip.

ROLLERS

● Rollers are ideal for painting large areas, particularly ceilings. There are several types of roller available to suit different paint jobs: foam, mohair or sheepskin in short, medium and long pile.

● Foam rollers are not recommended for normal emulsion paints as their spongy texture creates air bubbles in the paint film which then burst, leaving a cratered, orange-peel effect.

● A short-pile mohair roller is the most suitable for applying silk emulsion.

● A medium-pile sheepskin roller is ideal for applying matt emulsion.

● A medium- or long-pile roller is best for painting over textured surfaces, for example Artex ceilings and blown vinyl wall coverings.

● Solid emulsion paint comes in its own tray ready for application. A 17cm (7in) short-pile mohair roller is recommended.

● Some emulsion paints produces a subtly textured effect when applied with a short- or medium-pile roller or foam roller. Specially formulated for use on interior ceilings and walls, they will help to cover any minor surface imperfections.

● All rollers produce a 'mottled' surface and generally make more mess in terms of splatter and fly-off and it takes longer to clean up afterwards. However, rollers are quicker and easier to use.

AT THE END OF PAINTING

CLEANING BRUSHES AND ROLLERS

● To extend the life of your brushes and rollers, it is essential to clean them thoroughly and allow them to dry before storing.

● All brushes and rollers that have been used with water-based paints should be rinsed in cold water and then washed in warm water with a little detergent. Brushes used to apply solvent-based paints should be cleaned with a proprietary brush cleaner and renovator or white spirit and then washed in warm water with a little detergent.

● Rinse brushes in clean water, shake off excess water and wrap in a piece of clean paper towel, secured with masking tape. The brush will then dry back to its original shape, ready for the next job.

● Brushes should be stored flat. Standing brushes on their ends will bend the bristles and spoil them.

● Rollers should be stored hanging up to avoid crushing the pile.

● If you look after your brushes and rollers in this way they will last for years.

DISPOSING OF PAINT

● Waste paint can create problems if it is not disposed of correctly. The information on the back of the can will help you to work out the right amount of paint for the job. If you have any usable surplus, offer it to friends or to community groups who may be able to use it. Otherwise ask your local council for guidance – many do not want cans of paint disposed of in the dustbin. Never pour paint down the drain. Always put dried-out empty containers in the dustbin.

HINTS AND TIPS

● Keep pets and young children out of the way at all times when decorating.

● Make sure that step ladders are properly erected and positioned. Never try to over reach.

● If using a kitchen implement, such as a kitchen palette knife, to stir paint, it must be clearly labelled 'For paint stirring only' and not used again for any type of food preparation.

SPANISH BATHROOM

Finding Inspiration

Spain is a rich and diverse country with a beautiful landscape, stunning architecture and cultures, and also rich in history and tradition. The grandeur of the cities blends into countryside that varies from olive groves punctuating hard, red earth to fruit-laden vineyards that crisscross this fascinating land. Buildings may fade in the sunlight and even tumble down, but the spirit of the past is always preserved. This room aims to capture the traditional aspects of the Spanish way of life. Warm terracotta walls, blue and white hand-crafted tiles and distressed plaster façades all emphasize time-honoured values that are as important today as they have ever been. Natural sandstone colours and rich earthy reds remind us of the heat of the country and evoke images of dry, cracked earth and dusty pink tracks that wind down to the clearest turquoise-blue sea. This bathroom and its style echo the unhurried lifestyle of the Spanish people. There is no need to confront modernity here – the pitcher and bowl can be used as a basic shower unit, and a simple wicker food basket holds bathroom sponges, towels and loofahs.

COLOUR-WASHED WALLS

Colour washing is one of the easiest and most effective finishes for walls. The paint is applied to the surface using an ordinary decorators' brush and sponge. Wearing disposable gloves, simply 'wash' with a slightly thinned paint, a technique that is similar to that used for wiping the walls clean. It becomes just as easy to decorate your room as it does to spring clean! Continue to work around the walls quite quickly as it is important not to allow the leading paint edge to dry out. If you must take a break, finish painting one whole wall before taking a rest.

1

Prepare your walls prior to decoration (see page 5 for preparation details). Cover carpet or other floor coverings with a dust sheet and have a cloth handy for any drips. Apply the paler vinyl matt base colour to the walls using a decorators' brush or a medium-pile roller and a deep tray. As these walls are roughly plastered a brush was used to ensure an even coverage of paint.

2

Wearing disposable gloves, decant 500ml/1 pint of your warmer topcoat colour of vinyl matt paint into the well of a deep paint tray, add 100ml/4fl oz of tap water and mix together. Dip a decorators' sponge into the paint and apply to the walls using the scrubbing technique described in Hints and Tips (right). Be particularly careful at the corner point where the wall meets the ceiling.

HINTS AND TIPS

With colour washing you can create a cloudy, dappled look with softer layers of colours. For a finish like this, simply apply an uneven wash of colour using a broad decorators' brush over the first layer of thinned colour which will create a patchy effect. (When paint is thinned for colour washing it is very 'splashy' and will run up the handle of the brush so take extra care to cover floors well.) The cloudiness can be emphasized more strongly by applying three or four uneven washes of colour. Where there is only one layer of colour the walls will seem paler, and where there are two the colour acquires depth, building up a soft cloudy effect. The best way to achieve a colour-washed effect is by using a scrubbing technique with a sponge as if you were cleaning the walls. Stand away from the walls occasionally to assess the wash, applying more colour to areas that need more definition.

PAINTED TILE EFFECT

All around Spain you will notice the decorative blue and white tiles, often studded into roughly plastered walls in the cities. This feature is easily achieved using paint rather than real ceramic tiles, but the result is just as effective. Follow the step-by-steps, masking off the diamonds before colour washing, and you'll find it easy to paint this tile panel. Isolate the tiles illustrated or join the diamonds together, to create a room border at picture rail height or above the skirting board.

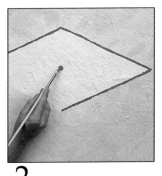

1

Position the template onto the wall using adhesive putty to hold it. Wearing disposable gloves, use the decorating sponge and the thinned topcoat emulsion wash to apply the paint around the template. Carefully remove the template to reveal the unpainted diamond underneath. Allow the washed colour to dry before continuing.

2

Still wearing gloves, tip a small amount of your chosen blue emulsion onto a paper plate or an old saucer. Use a fine artist's brush to paint in the tile border – you may need to add a little water to help the paint flow more easily. Then paint in the centre dot that will fix the position of the flowered tile pattern.

3

Paint in the centre flower using simple dashes of colour. Next paint in the scrolls either side of the flower. If you prefer, mark in this scroll with a pencil then paint over it. Move the template onto the next area and proceed as above. Follow these steps carefully to achieve a professional finish to your decorating.

HINTS AND TIPS

The size of the diamond tile panel is determined by the size of your own bathroom.

Be bold and paint large tiles rather than small ones for a dramatic effect. Use a retractable steel tape measure to measure your walls. It looks better if all the tiles are the same size, so measure your smallest wall first, as this will determine the size of the diamonds. Then cut a template from brown paper, and temporarily stick this onto the wall using spots of adhesive putty while you colour wash around it. To cut the diamond shape, first fold the paper into quarters. Draw in a quarter of the diamond, cut along the edge and unfold to reveal the paper template.

The wonderful warm, earthy feel of this Spanish bathroom can be easily emulated with just a few simple painting techniques.

The walls

This bathroom is airy and well ventilated so we have used a normal matt emulsion. However, if your bathroom is particularly prone to condensation, use colours from a range of paints specially formulated for kitchens and bathrooms, designed for use in areas where high levels of humidity and condensation are a problem. This will provide a hard-wearing, moisture-resistant satin finish and the special formulation gives an easy wipe-clean and grime-resistant surface that is ten times tougher than silk emulsion.

As the walls in the bathroom are thickly and, it must be said, roughly plastered, a decorators' brush rather than a roller was used to ensure that the paint went into every nook and cranny.

After the surface preparation apply a base coat of vinyl matt paint in your chosen colour. The soft wall wash that is applied over the base colour paint here is a mid-tone emulsion from a range of colours designed for interior use. These colours are ideal for highlighting key features of a room that would benefit from an accent colour, such as a window recess, behind shelves and above picture rails or below dado rails. In this case the paint is slightly thinned with a little tap water, in a ratio of five parts paint to one part water, and washed over the walls. Always add the water to the paint and mix together well. Use an old wooden ruler or kitchen palette knife to mix the paint thoroughly.

Colour-washing technique

The perfect technique for applying the topcoat wash onto the surface is to imagine that you are cleaning the walls. Apply the thinned paint with varying degrees of pressure so that the depth of colour is uneven, creating a mottled effect. Always stand back from your work from time to time to view the overall result. It's helpful to screw up your eyes to assess the build-up of colour and see the cloudy tones that you have applied. If you feel that the paint has become too strong in various areas, remove some of the colour by wiping with a clean, damp sponge. Remember to wear disposable gloves. Further degrees of cloudiness can be achieved by subsequently washing another, uneven layer of colour on top of the first one.

Tile design

The attractive tile design is painted straight onto the bare, whitewashed walls. A blue matt emulsion is used for the border and the pattern on the tile effect as only a small amount of colour is required. This intense shade of blue stands out vividly against the more neutral colour of the walls.

The woodwork

The woodwork in a bathroom should always be painted using a self-undercoating gloss paint which gives a durable yet fashionable finish. Alternatively, you could use a satinwood paint finish which has a matt appearance. It does not require an undercoat and contains Teflon for a tougher, hardwearing finish, making it ideal for use on interior woodwork as well as radiators.

Colour washing combinations

ITALIAN DINING ROOM

Finding Inspiration

An impressive array of stoneware surrounds the long dining table that is the centrepiece of this grand Italian-style room. The effect is heightened by copper urns, with an antique verdigris finish to create the appearance of years of damp and neglect. Windows on two sides of the room are opened to let in the balmy evening air. Wrought-iron chairs from the garden, quickly dusted down, add to the feeling of informality. Guests will dine from a menu of home-grown salad leaves – rocket, frisée and oak leaf – with sun-ripened cherry tomatoes and tiny new potatoes, dressed simply with fruity olive oil and pungent wine vinegar. As the sun lowers, the evening light dapples the softly textured walls displaying the warm sunny yellows at their best. A paint effect using one base colour and two sponged layers was applied to the roughly plastered walls, giving the wonderful mottled finish. The eye is then led downwards to the dado area. The stone blocking here is painted in exactly the same way as the walls, but the blocks are carefully marked in. Stone blocking is included in the overall decoration to break up the uniformity of the walls and to reinforce the illusion of a grand, Italian dining room.

STONE BLOCKING

Stone blocking can create a dramatic effect in a large area, such as a hallway, or in a more restricted space such as below the dado in this dining room. The characteristic block shapes are created by measuring lines that are then marked in chalk on top of the sponged wall finish. These are then painted in using a neutral-colour paint to resemble authentic 'grouting' lines, giving a bold stone blocking effect.

HINTS AND TIPS

Before starting to paint over carpeted areas or other floor coverings, cover everything with a dust sheet.

To simulate the 'grout' line that appears between the blocks it needs to be very narrow, approximately 1.25cm/½in. Using a ruler for accuracy, mark out all the blocks carefully with a pencil. Draw a chalk line onto the drawn lines and mark a line across the top of the blocking. Be very careful not to splash paint over the 'grout' lines and always keep a cloth handy to mop up any drips that might occur.

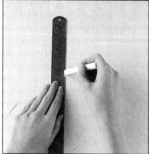

1

Paint the walls with the sponged wall finish as suggested on the opposite page. Work out the height of the stone blocking, then measure it. If your blocking is to be as low as this one you will only need two lines of blocks, so divide your measurement by two to give you each line's height. Draw in the horizontal lines with chalk. The width of each block is twice its height, so then draw in the vertical lines to create the blocks. Stagger them by drawing in the second line of blocks halfway along the first.

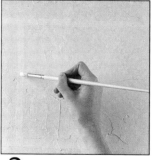

2

First decant a little of your 'grout' colour into a shallow dish or paint tray. You will only need a small amount of paint to cover an average sized room. With an artist's brush paint in the grout lines using faint chalk lines as your guide. Try to keep a steady hand as you progress the line. Then paint along the top of the horizontal chalk marks, and to the right of each vertical mark, not allowing the painted line to exceed 1.25cm/½in in width. Leave to dry then rub away any chalk marks that are left.

SPONGED WALL FINISH

Sponging is a wonderful paint technique for decorating enthusiasts and complete novices alike. It can be easily applied to the wall using one colour over a base coat, or using two sponged colours over a base colour as in this dining room. Ideally use a natural sponge or, if you prefer, the more environmentally friendly decorators' sponge. This can be sculpted into the right shape so that its finished print gives a natural effect.

1

Prepare the walls prior to decoration (see page 5 for preparation details). Here two coats of the base coat were used, and the paint was applied with a decorators' brush rather than a roller because of the roughly plastered texture underneath.

2

Prepare your sponge following the instructions in Hints and Tips (right). Wearing disposable gloves, decant a little of the first beige sponging colour into the well of a paint tray. Gently tip the tray so that the paint runs onto the sloping surface, then allow the paint to run back into the well. Dip your sponge into this layer of paint and apply it to the wall. Use a pecking motion to transfer the paint, altering the pattern by turning the sponge slightly each time you make a mark. Work the sponge over a small area, stand back to look at the effect, then fill in any gaps.

3

Once the first sponging colour has been applied, rinse out the paint tray and sponge. Squeeze excess water from the sponge and decant a little of the second, yellow sponging colour into the tray. Proceed as Step 2, tipping enough paint onto the tray's sloping surface before applying the colour. Use the same technique as before, overlapping the first sponged layer in some places but allowing both this and the base colour to show through in others. If the sponge becomes clogged, rinse, squeeze dry and continue.

HINTS AND TIPS

Natural sponges have different sized holes which create their delicate open texture. This can be imitated by sculpting a cellulose decorators' sponge, available from most decorating suppliers. They are yellow, rectangular, and about 5cm/2in thick, rather like bath sponges – but don't be tempted by this cheaper, inferior variety. Cut the sponge into half and then remove the smooth sides by pulling them away with your fingers. It doesn't matter if the sides tear raggedly as this is the effect we are after. Then pull small lumps from the surface of the sponge to create holes, varying the size to resemble a natural sponge. Test the print by pressing the dampened sponge into a little paint and dab onto some scrap paper with a pecking motion; add more holes if necessary to create the right effect.

To create the sunny scheme in this Italian dining room, paint the walls using two coats of the stone-coloured emulsion base colour. A large decorators' brush was used to apply the base coat because of the rough plaster on the walls, but you could use a roller on smooth walls. The subtle paint finish is vinyl soft sheen which brings warmth to interior painted walls.

Sponging the walls

The first colour used for the sponging layer was an attractive shade of beige in soft sheen and a sunny yellow was chosen as a second colour for the sponging. These were both chosen to coordinate with the selected neutral base colour.

When you start to sponge, it is important not to overload the sponge with paint as this may cause the paint to splodge onto the walls, rather than hold a definite printed mark. (You could practise this technique on some stiff white card beforehand.) If this does happen you should rinse the sponge under cold running water and squeeze the clean sponge until it is just moist, not wet, and begin where you left off.

Use a small piece of sponge to access tight corners or to work around window and door frames. Sculpt it to create a natural sponge effect (see Hints and Tips on previous page) and press onto the wall in the corner. If you are working around a corner it is best to do one side of the corner first then wait for this to dry (you could be working over the main part of the wall while this is drying) then sponge in the other side of the corner. This prevents the newly sponged area smudging when you apply paint on the second wall.

Apply the second colour in the same way as the first. In some areas you will seem to obliterate marks made by the first sponging layer, but there is no need to worry about this: the final effect will be softer and the sponged marks will create a decorative finish, unlike the cruder pattern of the first sponged coat.

The second layer of sponging really does transform the walls, but you will need to keep standing back to judge the application of paint. If any hint of a pattern starts to emerge, this will almost certainly be because you are not turning the sponge sufficiently after each mark is made. This does not have to be a big movement – just a small twist of the wrist will do – otherwise you could occasionally release the sponge, twist it through a 90-degree turn and use it the other way up. These are all clever tricks to make the overall, finished effect much more interesting.

Stone blocking

Once the sponged effect on the walls is dry you can add the stone block detailing. First mark out your blocks lightly onto the wall using white chalk. The lines will be quite faint but they will be sufficiently clear to follow as guidelines. Use an artist's brush to paint in the fine lines that will suggest the grouted area and give the characteristic stone block effect. You could use a brilliant white emulsion for a stronger grout line if you want your blocking to be dominant. But for a more subtle look, use the walls' base colour, as shown here.

The woodwork

The woodwork in this delightful room is painted using pure white satinwood, an oil-based alternative to gloss, with a matt finish. This provides a durable yet fashionable finish with a subtle satin sheen, it requires no undercoat and can be used on both interior woodwork and radiators.

Sponging colour combinations

AMERICAN STUDY

Finding Inspiration

New England is the inspiration for this study and its particular character is derived from a blend of English tradition and American innovation. Bold wood tones such as the natural wooden door and window frames help to bring a colonial feel to the room. A simple *trompe l'oeil* technique is used to emulate the impressive panelling often found in homes around this beautiful part of America. This cost-effective solution is easy to achieve using emulsion paints – all you need is a little patience to plot the panels with chalk and then paint them in. The tranquillity of this room need not be disturbed by bright lighting. The flicker of an open-wood fire or natural light, filtered through American-style blinds, will give enough light to both read and relax by. To complete the study's charm, add furniture that embodies the area's style. Look for traditionally made wooden furniture, particularly pieces with metal angle supports and hinges. A grandfather clock and a winged armchair complete the look and, although they originate in eighteenth-century England, they are also New England style and help create the relaxed, Anglo-American ambience of the room.

SIMPLE *TROMPE L'OEIL* PANELLING

Trompe l'oeil is the 'trick of the eye' paint technique that gives a three-dimensional effect. Here, a simplified panel is first drawn onto the wall with white chalk and then painted using two pale blue colours to give a simple two-tone effect. This method is ideal to use in a bedroom or dining room as well as in a study.

HINTS AND TIPS

Always ensure that there are whole panels along the length of one wall. To do this, measure and plot the panels for each wall independently. Aim to make the size of the panels equal for each wall, although of course the panels may need to be slightly larger on one wall or smaller on another in order to fit whole panels along the length.

Begin working on the wall with the most unbroken space, rather than those with window and door frames, alcoves or radiators. Measure the length of each wall and subtract from this figure the widths of the panels. Divide this measurement by the number of gaps between panels, for example six panels will need seven gaps. The remaining figure indicates the width of each gap.

Chalk is an ideal marker as it is easily removed after painting or if mistakes are made.

1

Prepare the walls prior to decoration (see page 5 for preparation details). Using a ruler, measure the length of the wall and determine the panel widths and the gaps in between (see Hints and Tips, left). Use chalk and a long ruler to plot the panel onto the wall. The painted strip that forms the side of each panel should be approximately 2.5cm/1in thick. If your walls are very uneven, it is best to use a spirit level to help you maintain the true verticals and horizontals.

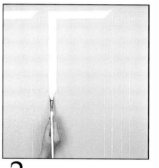

2

Choose two pale shades of blue, making sure that one is considerably lighter than the other. First paint in the darker of the two shades, using an artist's brush to maintain an even thickness. Paint along the top of the panel and then continue down the left edge. Then paint a diagonal line at the top right and bottom left corners so that a neat mitre is formed.

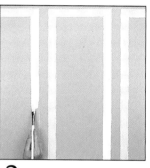

3

Paint the lighter blue colour along the remaining two sides of the panel, again maintaining an even thickness with the artist's brush. You will start to see the trompe l'oeil effect taking place as the lighter part of the panelling appears to reflect more light. The darker side seems to recede and it is this effect that creates the overall three-dimensional look.

BRUSHWOOD EFFECT ON A JUNK CHAIR

Forget the mess and hassle of paint projects of the past – this effect can easily be created in any home with a two-part paint, such as Brushwood from Dulux, which transforms any painted wooden surface and gives it the look of natural wood. No stripping back or hours of tedious sanding is necessary. The treatment is simple: apply one or two coats of base coat over the old painted surface, and finish with one or two layers of top coat.

1

This chair was bought from a junk shop, but you can easily find similar ones at car boot sales and second-hand shops, or you may have a painted chair at home just waiting for a new lease of life. Prepare the wood by sanding with fine sandpaper (sanding in the direction of the grain), and then give it a quick wipe to remove all the dust.

2

To make painting easier, stand the chair on a protected table top. Paint on the base coat of the two-part treatment and brush out any paint that drips along the spindles at the back of the chair or forms small pools of paint at their base.

3

Sand the surface lightly once the base coat has dried. Apply the top coat, and follow the direction of the natural wood grain to create a more authentic look. A thinner coat will give a more realistic appearance than a thicker one. Leave to dry thoroughly. Make a second application of the top coat if you require a deeper finish.

HINTS AND TIPS

As with all paint, do not be tempted to skimp on the drying time between coats. Ideally try and leave the chair to dry overnight.

This wood-effect paint treatment has endless potential around the home. Any previously painted surface can be transformed, from dado rails and skirting boards to picture rails and doors. Then you can progress to trunks, chests, chairs, front doors, window frames and so on – once you have started, no piece of wood will ever look the same again!

The walls

For this American study the walls above the dado rail were painted with a subtly textured emulsion paint that brings an interesting texture to the decor while covering any minor wall imperfections. Used here in magnolia, it is a warmer alternative to the smooth conventional emulsion finish andgives excellent coverage. This textured paint can be applied using a short- or medium-pile roller or a foam roller. It is less messy to use as it tends to splatter less than ordinary emulsion during roller application.

To contrast with the magnolia paint colour that was used on the walls above the dado rail, a Wedgwood blue was applied to the area below it. A vinyl soft sheen was applied here, for a medium sheen effect which is ideal for highlighting key features around a room such as below a dado.

The panelling

For the panelling itself, two shades of pale blue were chosen. As only a small amount of paint was required for each colour, all that was needed were the 250ml tester pots. Satinwood was used for the blue-painted woodwork in the dado rail itself as well as for the wooden skirting board.

The natural wood surfaces were treated with a woodstain and varnish in light oak. This was used to stain and protect the door, its frame, the window shutters and window frame. The special formula is very tough and hardwearing, so when applied to woodwork it provides excellent resistance to any knocks, dents or scratches. It stains and protects all interior and exterior smooth planed wood in one.

Brushwood from Dulux was used to revitalize the old chair. Its special formula enables you to paint over a previously painted surface with minimal preparation, and the finished top coat gives the natural look of wood grain. This is an easy to apply two-part process comprising a special base coat and top coat.

Creating a panelled effect

INDIAN LIVING ROOM

Finding Inspiration

Indian colours are as rich and vibrant as the country itself. Strong, fiery reds, ochre, cinnabar and orange all vie for attention, yet these colours combine together brilliantly and the effect they create is breathtaking. Strong colours in a room are inspiring and these spicy Indian tones are no exception. Colours are 'rubbed' into each other almost haphazardly and this produces an exquisite finish and a depth of colour that could be straight out of the cities of Jaipur or Bombay.

From the bold architecture of the Taj Mahal to remote rural villages, colour influences the very spirit of India. Bright markets, attractive courtyards, detailed fretwork screens, printed saris and cooking pots are all natural elements of the country that give it its unique style. The walls of this inviting Indian-inspired living room have been painted in a pinky-mauve colour and overlaid with a soft, spicy pink to give a strong, dappled effect. The decorative teardrop pattern, inspired by the classic paisley motif, is applied with a gloved forefinger to create an authentic Indian effect.

LIMERICK LIBRARY

Step-by-Step

COLOUR-RUBBED WALLS

If you have only just come around to thinking that you can paint with a sponge, then you may think it's a crazy idea to start painting with a cloth. However, this painting technique has created some of the glorious finishes seen in many homes and interior magazines today. Colour rubbing with soft toning colours can create a gentle, dappled quality, whereas the effect of the strong colours here is rich and vibrant. A border is created just above skirting level allowing the base colour to show through the top colour, and a row of hand-painted dots separates the rubbed colour from the border.

HINTS AND TIPS
Use a large piece of lightweight material such as some cotton muslin for the colour rubbing. Never use artificial fabric or the type of cloth used to wipe floors, or any fabric such as wool that would deposit fibres over your paintwork. Wearing disposable gloves, apply the paint using a rubbing motion, allowing a little of the base colour to show through. Once the cloth has become saturated with paint, throw it away and use a fresh one. Expect to use at least six cloths for an average-sized room.

1

Prepare the walls prior to decoration (see page 5 for preparation details). Use a medium-pile roller to apply the base coat to the walls. A cranberry shade was used here for the base colour. Cover with one or two coats of the base colour, allowing the first layer to dry thoroughly before applying the second. Use a small decorators' brush to paint the corners and around the door and window frames.

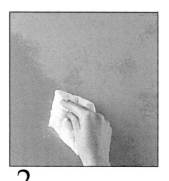

2

Pour 500ml/1 pint of top coat paint into the well of a paint tray and add 100ml/¼ pint of clean tap water. Mix the paint with an old wooden ruler or kitchen palette knife, then use a tape measure and pencil to determine the height of the border at floor level. Measure up about 5cm/2in from the skirting board and, using a long ruler, lightly draw in the border with a chalked line. Rub the paint onto the wall's surface and work around the whole room.

3

Wearing disposable gloves, dip your forefinger into a small tester pot of your chosen highlight colour and apply a dot where the rubbed colour meets the solid base colour. Keep doing this until the line is filled with tiny dots of colour. Don't worry if the dots are irregular shapes or if they are spaced unevenly because this is part of the finished effect. As long as you stay close to the painted border the dots will not waver too much.

PAISLEY WALL DECORATION

The original paisley patterns were based upon plant forms, and the teardrop shapes detailed here are based on these designs. A template is cut from the pattern on this page and positioned on the walls using a little adhesive putty. The dots of colour are once again applied with the gloved forefinger and they may be painted around the template once, twice or even three times to vary the look of the overall pattern.

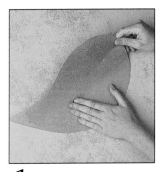

1

Stick the paper template directly onto the wall using adhesive putty. You will need to use three or so pieces so that the sides of the template do not fold inwards. Use your imagination when positioning the template around the room – twist it in different directions so that the paisley pattern looks more interesting when seen from a distance, and occasionally position it upside down and paint around it.

2

Use dots of colour to 'draw' around the shape. Once the outline is painted, remove the paper template and progress onto another shape, or paint a second outline of dots to emphasize the existing ones. Follow the outline around the inside or the outside of the shape. With adhesive putty, tack the template onto the walls at random and keep standing back from the work to make sure there is not a build-up of pattern in one area.

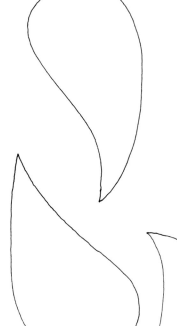

HINTS AND TIPS

Scale up the drawing on this page to make a template for the wall and cut the resulting template from brown paper. Some of the paisley patterns may be painted in at random, provided you feel you have the confidence to paint onto the walls directly, otherwise make up a series of approximately five or six teardrop shapes. When making your template it is advisable to cut five or six extras to use in case paint smudges onto the back of the original.

When you have prepared your walls ready for decoration (see page 5) you can then apply one or two coats of your chosen base colour in vinyl matt, using a medium-pile emulsion roller. The perfect base colour for the colour-rubbed walls in this Indian-style room is a mauvy-pink.

To create the softly rubbed colour effect, you need to fold the ends of the cotton cloth into the centre and gather it up as if you were about to start cleaning the walls. Dilute the paint used in the paint tray with a proportion of one part clean tap water to five parts paint. Mix thoroughly using an old wooden ruler or a kitchen palette knife. Dip the cloth directly into the paint but be careful not to overload it.

Apply the colour on top of the base coat with a light circular motion as if you were cleaning the walls. Some harder imprints will be left on the surface of the base colour where the crumpled edges of the cloth have deposited a little paint. Leave these, as they are an intrinsic part of the overall paint finish. If you decide that you want to use lighter colours, it works best if you just apply one base coat to the walls. When this is dry you can colour-rub two further top coats. Using more top coats will soften the overall effect, while fewer make it more prominent.

A softer, subtle finish can be achieved if you apply a dilute white emulsion layer on top of the first rubbed colour. Follow the step-by-step instructions as outlined and apply this wash as an addition to Step 2. Mix together equal quantities of brilliant white emulsion and water to produce a thin, dilute colour, but be very careful when you apply the paint as it will be very thin and 'splashy'. Use the same technique, rubbing the colour onto the walls with a cotton cloth. The thin wash will soften the underlying colour. Still try to maintain an unevenness, as with the previous layer, so that the base coat and first rubbed layer of colour show through. Make sure that the floor is completely covered with a dust sheet before you start, as this diluted colour is very thin. You will also need to have a cloth handy, to wipe up any errant drips or splashes that have occurred.

All the woodwork in the Indian living room was painted in satinwood, using a similar shade to that of the walls.

Colour rubbing
combinations

ENGLISH BEDROOM

Finding Inspiration

Straight out of a summer garden, this room brings to mind newly mown lawns, abundant herbaceous borders, the crack of a cricket ball meeting willow, fragrant tea roses, cucumber sandwiches, strawberries and clotted cream. The wonderful images that conjure up an English midsummer are glorious but hazy – happily

anticipated as June becomes July and preparations are made to re-string old tennis rackets and dust down the wicker picnic hamper. Then, all too soon the tennis season is over, August has run into September, autumn creeps in, and the forecasted Indian summer does not happen.

The colour scheme shown here is an attempt to capture the perfection of an English summer, when the all too fleeting elements are in our favour, and hold it within four walls forever. Broad vertical stripes have been softened with a thinned white emulsion paint, giving a delicate chalky finish to a base colour that would otherwise be too dominant on such a scale. The eye is then led downward to a filigree border that decorates the area above the skirting board.

Step-by-Step

CHALKY STRIPED WALLS

The beauty of this wall finish belies its simplicity. Wide stripes are first plotted around the room using a plumb line ,then painted in, either as shown here, or as broad or narrow as you wish. A steady hand is not necessarily an advantage, because the edges are softened afterwards with a broad brush and thinned white emulsion. The end result is a cost-effective alternative to wallpaper, that is easy to achieve and always gets perfect results.

HINTS AND TIPS

A plumb line or a spirit level is indispensable for setting the verticals. Don't be tempted to use a tape or a ruler without a plumb line, as the slightest bump on the walls will throw the line out. A home-made plumb line using string and a small weight, such as a cotton reel, will have the desired effect. Let the plumb line settle, then fix to the wall with adhesive putty and draw in the line with chalk. If you have a picture rail, don't let the stripes go above it because they will begin to look like checks. Instead, paint this area a solid colour and then use the same wash treatment with some thinned emulsion. The best way of colour washing is by using a scrubbing technique with a brush as if you were cleaning the walls. Stand away from the walls occasionally to assess the wash, adding more colour to areas that need definition.

1

Prepare the walls prior to decoration (see page 5 for preparation details). If you are using a spirit level hold it against the wall where the first stripe will begin and lightly mark the vertical drop with a pencil or chalk. A plumb line should be held at the top of the wall where each stripe begins, at either ceiling or picture rail height. Determine the width of the stripes and mark this around the top of the wall, moving the plumb line along and drawing in the verticals as before.

2

Before painting, cover the floor with a dust sheet to protect it from thinned paint. Use a large decorators' brush to paint in the alternative stripes with the pink emulsion. Brush slightly beyond the pencil lines to cover the drawn line. Brush the emulsion vertically, in long broad strokes, following the stripes. Finish the ends of each stripe by brushing the emulsion paint close to the edge of the ceiling and skirting board using a smaller decorators' brush. Leave to dry.

3

Prepare the brilliant white wash in a paint kettle, adding one part water to one part paint, and stir this together using an old wooden ruler or kitchen palette knife to ensure the paint is thoroughly mixed. Dip a large decorators' brush into the wash and rub it against the paint kettle to remove excess paint. Apply to the painted stripes and again, as in Step 1, always brush in the direction of the stripes. Catch any drips with the ends of the brush and paint back into the wash. Allow to dry thoroughly.

Step-by-Step

STENCILLED BORDER

Stencilling allows you to embellish a room artistically, but without too much effort. Once the initial cutting of the stencil is complete, it's plain sailing – yet the results can be stunning. You can use Manila paper, as shown here, or an acetate stencilling sheet. Both are available from artists' suppliers. Small tester pots of paint colour are ideal for this kind of decoration.

1

Photocopy the image to a size that suits your room. If your bedroom is not too big then you may choose to have a slightly smaller border, but remember that as the decoration is low, at skirting level, the stencil is always more effective on a larger scale. To cut out the intricate details of the design, fix with adhesive putty onto the stencil card to hold in place. Also use small spots of the putty on the reverse of the stencil card and fix close to the cut edges to ensure that the stencil is placed close to the wall.

2

Fix stencil in place. Tip a little of the two colours with a small amount of white emulsion onto a palette – a paper plate is ideal. Use a clean brush for each colour. Dip the ends of the stencil brush into one colour and dab off the excess onto scrap paper. Stencil the design, occasionally picking up a little white emulsion to add variation to the colour. When complete, peel back the stencil and repeat the process. Always reposition the stencil using the registration marks and keep the back of the stencil clean.

HINTS AND TIPS

The template on this page can be enlarged under a photocopier until you have a bold, oversized stencil that suits your room. Join the sheets of photocopies together with clear tape, use adhesive putty to fix to the stencil card, and cut out the shaded areas of the design using a very sharp craft knife on a cutting mat, if you have one, or a piece of glass, but not the coffee table! To maintain an even cutting line try not to lift the blade more than is necessary. Cut the small details first then work from the centre outwards. In order to continue the stencilled design around the room, the stencil has registration marks – these are parts of the design that fit directly over the last pattern repeat. If you accidentally cut through or break one of the stencil bridges, it should be repaired with masking tape and re-cut. It is a good idea to make some spare stencils, especially if using Manila pape,r as paint may accidentally smudge onto the back of the original and transfer to the wall. Alternatively, any smudges can be wiped off carefully with a damp sponge.

The techniques for achieving the look of this English bedroom are gloriously simple. If you already have white emulsioned walls, then you are halfway there – these walls will only require a quick coat of white emulsion. Apply emulsion paint with a roller for effortless coverage.

If your walls have been painted with any other colour, then we recommend that you use two coats of brilliant white emulsion.

For the perfect base for the chalky pink stripes, all you have to do is choose the finish: vinyl matt is ideal for disguising a wall's imperfections and giving a rich matt finish; vinyl silk provides a silky finish to interior walls and is easily wiped clean; vinyl soft sheen has a subtle finish, bringing softness and warmth to walls. Vinyl soft sheen is more washable than matt, and less shiny than vinyl silk. Choose the finish that suits your lifestyle, but remember to use the same finish in the brilliant white for the chalky wash.

Plot the stripes following the steps outlined. You will need a strong base colour so that, once the wash is applied, the original colour still has the intensity to show through.

Choose the brilliant white emulsion – vinyl matt, vinyl silk or vinyl soft sheen – to partner the base colour, and thin this with an equal quantity of water, stirring well to ensure it is thoroughly mixed, but be very careful when you apply the paint as it is so thin and 'splashy'.

Applying the wash is one of the best parts of the painting process. Not only is it fast, but the thin veil of emulsion subtly transforms the strong pink accent colour to give a truly professional effect. Before you start, protect the floors with a dust sheet and always use a cloth to wipe up any drips.

For the stencilled border, small tester pots of paint can be used, as only a small amount of paint is needed. The pink and green shades chosen here are perfect for a really bold design where the emphasis is on maximum colour. These colours look wonderfully mellow all year round in the artificial light of evening, but still keep fresh and crisp in the early morning sun.

The natural wood floorboards are easily treated with a quick-drying, water-based varnish. This is touch-dry in 30 minutes and re-touchable in two hours. Available in gloss, satin and matt finishes, it has polyurethane to help withstand knocks and spills.

Washed-stripe colour
combinations

FRENCH KITCHEN

Finding Inspiration

You can almost feel the soft, dappled sunlight filtering through the dusty wooden shutters and smell the invigorating aroma of rich, fresh coffee in the timeless tranquillity of this French country kitchen. Simple glass pots are filled with fruity conserves made from home-grown cherries, plums and sweet myrtles. This kitchen is the foundation of the home. It hides the necessary modern appliances behind roll-up wicker blinds, and displays the attractive accessories – an age-worn cheese safe, ancient weighing scales and an iron hanging rack. The dappled hues on the wall do not solely rely on the Provençal sunshine for their delicate sunlight patterns – the interior is cleverly painted using vibrant, sunny colours. The walls are deceptively easy to paint. The thin veils of colour suggesting a glorious decorative quality are actually mixtures of thinned paint, brushed over a solid base coat. The paint is applied using a scrubbing motion with the brush, a technique not out of place during a painting session with the under-fives, but executed in a controlled manner to give these superb results.

Step-by-Step

COLOUR-WASHED WALLS

A whole room can be transformed with this wonderfully easy painting technique in a matter of hours. The great thing about washing your walls with colour in this way is that you can add more pigment to the walls little by little, until you achieve the effect you are happy with. These kitchen walls were colour washed using two main colours, then subtle patches of a darker hue were added to give more depth and character.

HINTS AND TIPS

The colour wash was applied with a broad decorators' brush using matt emulsion paint that had been thinned. As the paint is watery, remember to cover the floor with a dust sheet and keep a cloth handy for drips.

The best effects are achieved by brushing the colour thinly. Allow some base colour to show through in some areas but not in others, to build up a cloudy colour. Pale colour washes can be applied over a white base coat, but darker and mid-tone colours, seen here, are best painted over a coloured base coat.

1

Prepare the walls prior to decorating (see page 5 for preparation details). Use a medium-pile roller and deep tray to apply two layers of the pale yellow base coat, allowing the first coat to dry before applying the second. Tip 500ml/1 pint of the paler yellow colour into a paint kettle and add 100ml/4 fl oz of cold tap water. Stir well with an old wooden ruler or kitchen palette knife. Use a decorators' brush to apply the wash to the walls.

2

Prepare the second wash by tipping 250ml/10 fl oz of pure white kitchen and bathroom paint into a paint kettle and adding 250ml/10 fl oz of cold water. Once again, use the brush to apply the paint onto the walls using the same scrubbing technique as before over the first washed layer. Because the wash has a larger proportion of water to paint, you may find that it starts to run. Simply catch the drips and brush them back into the walls. Allow some of the base colour and the first washed colour to show through the paint.

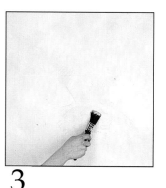

3

Once the white cloudy layer has dried, you may wish to add an extra wash. This really adds character and charm to the paint finish and is well worth the extra effort. Mix together 100ml/4 fl oz of a slightly darker hue with 100ml/4 fl oz of clean water in the same way as before and use a small decorators' brush to rub the colour into the walls. Apply this beige colour selectively, particularly around the door and window frames. Stand back from the walls and view the paint finish, adding only small areas of this top colour where necessary.

DISTRESSED CHAIR AND TABLE

This effect is achieved by sanding down, or 'distressing', painted layers to give the impression of ageing. This chair and table were rescued from a junk shop, relieved of their thick layers of old paint and varnish and given a whole new lease of life. A collection of not-quite-matching 'distressed' chairs could be complemented with a scrubbed pine kitchen table as the first steps to creating the perfect kitchen with an authentic, country feel.

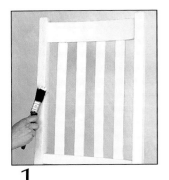

1

Prepare the chair for painting (see Hints and Tips, right) and wipe down the surface to ensure it is completely dust-free. Use a small decorators' brush to paint the chair with one layer of the creamy base colour. Brush the paint onto the surface smoothly and evenly, not allowing the paint to well up between the vertical slats on the seat back.

2

When the first colour is completely dry, use a fine grade sandpaper lightly to prepare the surface for the second colour. Apply an even coat of the second sea-blue colour over the paler first coat, making sure that you completely cover the base colour. As the chair dries, keep checking for any slight drips and brush these into the paint.

3

Allow the chair to dry thoroughly then start to distress the paint layers. Use the abrasive paper with a sanding block on the larger flatter areas and tear off small pieces to access the tricky corners. A fine sandpaper was used on this chair and table as it is more efficient on the smooth painted surface.

HINTS AND TIPS

Take time to remove all the old varnish from the woodwork. If the woodwork is already painted, first rub the surface with a medium then a fine sandpaper to provide a base for the new colour. If your piece of furniture has been taken back to the wood you will need to prime this before painting (see preparation details, page 5).

Allow each coat to dry thoroughly before applying the next one. Let the paint dry completely, preferably overnight, before sanding down. Use the labour-intensive sanding block and paper method to distress the paint. Traditional colours were used for these chairs, but different effects can be achieved by changing the colours. To work on the chair, stand it on a table top covered in newspaper to make it easier to paint the legs.

The step-by-step techniques for creating the French kitchen can be achieved with minimum effort. The finished result, however, is a superb country kitchen that has maximum style. The distressed finish on the kitchen chair adds a unique charm to otherwise ordinary woodwork, lifting it from the downright dull to something worthy of display. Designers often incorporate a piece of distressed furniture, be it a chair, a wall cabinet or a table, into their design plans, as it gives the impression of a more interesting, mysterious past.

The glorious dappled colour of these softly colour-washed walls was achieved using a pale yellow vinyl matt which forms a good, solid base colour. The base colour was applied using a medium-pile roller and deep paint tray. For an expert finish, put on two coats of the base colour, allowing the first coat to dry thoroughly before you apply the second.

The first layer of colour wash used was a sunny yellow in a satin-finish paint specially formulated for kitchens and bathrooms. It is necessary to add a small amount of water to the colour in order to brush the paint out thinly onto the surface of the walls – the idea is to gradually build up an uneven layer of patchy, cloudy colour using a scrubbing technique with the brush.

For the second 'wash', white kitchen and bathroom paint was mixed with a little tap water, as above. The white emulsion helps provide a thin veil of colour over the first layer of the colour wash, transforming the stronger colour, making the paint finish much softer and blending in the hard brush strokes to bring a subtle, chalky effect to the walls.

The final colour which is applied over the second layer of colour wash is an optional one. If you are delighted with the results after this second layer then stop, but if you wish to add some delicate lowlights to the wall then use the same washing technique to apply a third colour sparingly around the room. Thinned paint in a darker shade of beige was used in this scheme.

If your kitchen is prone to high levels of condensation or humidity, then it is a good idea to use only paints that have been specially formulated for use in kitchens and bathrooms, including the paint for the base coat.

Colour-washing
combinations

SCANDINAVIAN LIVING ROOM

Finding Inspiration

Cool, understated and very sophisticated, the Scandinavian living room is a relaxed place in which to contemplate, rest and unwind from the pressures of the day. Bleached wood and scrubbed limewashed floors are typical features of Scandinavian style. Think of crisp cotton lace on a translucent white marble tabletop and you can begin to appreciate the subtleties of white upon white: a delicate ivy leaf, iced like frosted fruit in a winter garden, gossamer spiders' webs, dewy in the coolness of an early autumn morning, or an exhaled breath captured in cold, icy air. There are many tones of white – inspirational whites that are straight from nature itself, or whites that we find in our own homes. Freshly laundered linen, peaks of soft fluffy meringue and even the crystalline spheres of a mothball all retain individual textures and tones of a unifying white. Floor-to-ceiling panels in this scheme are painted boldly onto the walls and then decorated with a 'twisting leaf' design which twines around a finely painted edge that lies very close to the panelling borders.

Step-by-Step

DECORATIVE PANELS

The beauty of these panels lies in the clever overlaying of different tones of white. A very pale, pink-tinged white is used as a base coat for the two other shades. The secret lies in the application of the final lilac-tinged white, which should be thinned slightly to reveal a little of the underlying colour. Use five parts paint to one part water, and paint with the brush using vertical strokes.

HINTS AND TIPS

To make sure that the panels are evenly spaced, decide on the number of panels you need to paint onto one wall, then use a retractable tape measure to measure the width of the wall. Subtract the widths of the panels, then divide the remaining measurement by the number of spaces required between the panels – for example, three panels would require four spaces. You can then use this final measurement as the width of each gap to plot the position of each panel. Work out each wall separately so that you have panels across every side of the room.

You will need to use a plumb line to set the verticals on the wall before you start to paint in the panelling, or you could make your own by using a small weight tied to one end of a piece of string. Suspend the plumb line from the top of the wall and mark the verticals lightly with chalk or pencil.

1

Prepare the walls prior to decoration (see page 5 for preparation details). Apply two coats of the pale base colour with a roller. Mark the panels onto the wall as described in Hints and Tips (left), using a long piece of wood to draw in the horizontals. Then paint inside the panels using the lilac-tinged white that has been slightly thinned (five parts paint to one part water). Using a decorators' brush, apply the chosen vinyl matt paint to the panel exteriors, remembering to paint across the horizontals to form long rectangular panels.

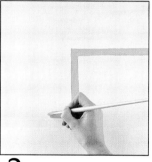

2

To paint the fine lining of the panel in a pale sage green emulsion, use a ruler and draw chalk lines to guide you. The line is painted 2.5cm/1in in from the edge of the border and is 2.5cm/1in wide. To create the angled corners, make a square paper template and use adhesive putty to fix this into each corner successively.

Step-by-Step

TWISTING LEAF MOTIF

This attractive decoration is painted on top of the fine-lined edge. Although it looks like a freehand painted design it is in fact a repeated pattern that is easily reproduced with the help of some tracing paper. Simply outline the printed design, and move the motif around the edges of the border. Then remove to reveal the outline decoration on the walls, and paint!

1

Trace the decorative leaf from this page and enlarge the design under a photocopier as described in Hints and Tips (right). Place a sheet of tracing paper over the photocopied image and trace the outline. Reverse the tracing paper and position over the painted line. Then carefully outline the image with a pencil so that the image is transferred onto the wall.

2

Using a fine artist's brush, paint inside the pencil lines. As the leafy edge meets the angled corner you may only need to use a part of the design to fill around the border. Once you are familiar with the pattern you may feel confident enough to fill in these small areas freehand without using the template.

HINTS AND TIPS

Once you have drawn around the motif on this page you can always enlarge the design under a photocopier until the length of the twist measures 45cm/18in. Use a soft pencil to outline the motif on tracing paper. When you have transferred the image onto the wall, use a soft eraser to thin down the outline. Make sure your pencil marks are very light, or they may show through the paint.

The Professional Touch

Although this spectacular panelling will certainly be a focal point in any room, it really lends itself to the scale of a room normally associated with the living area. It takes a little longer to achieve than some of the other techniques outlined in this book, but the stunning results are well worth the extra effort. The final effect may show very little of the underlying base coat, yet this is an important colour because it shows through the thinned, second coat. Matt colours were used to decorate the Scandinavian living room as this type of paint is  perfectly suited to the limewashed floorboards, table and chairs which furnish the room. A subtle pink colour was chosen to create a perfect base coat for the panelling.

To apply the paint, use a medium-pile roller and deep tray for good coverage. A small decorators' brush is useful to paint around the door and window frames and into the corners. Plot the panels carefully, measuring then calculating each wall separately. You will need to dilute the top coats so that these can be brushed out quite thinly inside the panelled area. Always add water to the paint, never add paint to the water otherwise you may start to find some lumps forming. It is also easier to decant the paint into a paint kettle and add the water from a measuring jug.

Stir the paint thoroughly until the water is mixed in. Use the paint directly from the paint kettle and, to keep the dilution of paint consistent, mix a second batch of colour only when the first has completely run out. Use a decorators' brush to paint the diluted colour inside the panelled area. Brush in the paint using vertical strokes and allow some patches of the underlying pink to show through.

A sage green was used for the fine lining, and the delicate leafy details of the pattern were painted using a smoky blue. As only a small amount of colour is used, a small tester pot will be sufficient.

Use two coats of satinwood to paint all the woodwork; this can also be used as the finish on the radiators. Classic white would suit the colour scheme in this room.

When using solvent-based paints inside, ensure you have good ventilation. Keep doors and windows fully open during painting and drying: this will make the application less unpleasant and reduce the characteristic just-painted smell. Do not use solvent-based products on large surface areas inside, or in small confined spaces. If you mistakenly paint onto the glass, wait until this is dry, then scrape it off with a sharp craft blade or a window scraper.

LIMERICK COUNTY LIBRARY

A Buyer's Guide to Dulux Paints

Dulux Kitchens & Bathrooms paint is specially formulated to be moisture-resistant in areas susceptible to condensation (it is not suitable for areas that are regularly soaked with water, for example shower enclosures). **Dulux** Kitchens & Bathrooms paint has an attractive satin finish which means it is easier to clean than ordinary emulsion paints and is ten times tougher than conventional silk emulsion, to help keep your walls looking good for much longer.

Flexicover from **Dulux** is specially formulated to fill and cover hairline cracks in ceilings. Because it is flexible it will then keep cracks covered. **Flexicover** from **Dulux** is much cleaner for roller use than ordinary emulsion paint, with minimal splatter. **Flexicover** from **Dulux** is also suitable for interior walls.

Dulux Vinyl Matt is a rich matt finish, which subtly enhances the beauty of your walls. Its new, tougher formulation, which is easily washable, will keep your room looking like new for a long time.

Dulux Vinyl Soft Sheen gives walls a beautiful subtle sheen, bringing softness and warmth to your home. Less shiny than silk, soft sheen is a hardwearing and scuff-resistant finish.

Dulux Vinyl Silk is a smooth silk finish, which gives a delicate shine to walls and is hardwearing and scuff-resistant.

Dulux Once Emulsion comes in a vinyl soft sheen finish especially formulated to cover in one coat. Available in 19 inspirational colours, plus white, it is designed to suit any colour scheme. A complementary range of colours is also available in Once Gloss.

Dulux Solid Emulsion can be spread straight from the tray with little splatter or mess. Pure Brilliant White **Dulux** Solid Emulsion gives a crisp, bright look and creates an open and fresh feeling.

Natural Hints from **Dulux** is a range of emulsion paints with a delicate hint of colour. **Natural Hints** from **Dulux** create a light and soft effect to co-ordinate beautifully with the interior of your home.

Naturals is a range of six calm contemporary colours echoing the fashion for natural textures and fabrics such as wicker, linen, hessian and calico, to enable you to create the natural look in your home. Available in Vinyl Matt, Vinyl Soft Sheen and Vinyl Silk finishes.

Special Effects from **Dulux** is a range of semi-transparent, water-based paints in a range of attractive toning colours, designed to help you create beautiful and unique paint effects such as sponging, rag rolling, graining, stippling and dragging quickly and easily. Special Effects can be applied over emulsion, satinwood or gloss and used on walls, woodwork and furniture.

Pure Brilliant White from **Dulux** gives a crisp, bright look and creates a fresh, spacious feeling.

Dulux coloured emulsions offer a range of shades to suit any colour scheme; the colours are specially designed to blend and tone together.

Dulux Once Gloss has been specially developed by ICI to give a unique combination of convenience, performance, toughness and superior top coat.

Dulux Non-Drip Gloss is easy to use, as it resists drips and runs and does not require an undercoat. **Dulux** Non-Drip Gloss is suitable for use both inside and outside on wood and metal surfaces, including radiators. It gives long lasting beauty as well as protection.

Dulux Satinwood is a beautiful satin finish specially designed for use on interior wood and metal, including radiators. It is a subtle, attractive alternative to gloss but just as hard wearing and washable. **Dulux** Satinwood is drip-resistant and easy to use. It needs no undercoat and can be applied directly over old gloss paint after preparation.

Dulux Undercoat is the ideal partner for **Dulux** Gloss Finish. It has superb hiding power, good 'cling' to sharp edges and excellent levelling properties. **Dulux** Undercoat can be used inside and out, with **Dulux** Gloss Finish and an appropriate **Dulux** primer, for the perfect gloss paint system.

Dulux Gloss Finish is a rich gloss paint which flows out to give a perfect mirror-like finish. Use it inside and out on wood and metal surfaces to give long-lasting protection and beauty to your home.

Dulux Water-Based Gloss is ideal for use on interior and exterior wood. With its low-odour, quick drying formulation, it is convenient and pleasant to use. **Dulux** Water-Based Gloss is drip resistant and does not require an undercoat. Brushes can be cleaned with water. **Dulux** Water-Based Gloss is not suitable for use on heated surfaces, i.e. radiators. Newly painted doors and windows should not be closed (tightly) until the paint is fully dry.

Dulux Colour Palette contains over 600 colours, mixed to order. The range is available in a wide variety of finishes: Vinyl Matt, Vinyl Silk, Vinyl Soft Sheen, Gloss, Satinwood and Weathershield Smooth Masonry Paint.

Dulux Woodsheen is a superior woodstain and varnish that colours and protects all in one. It has a long-lasting satin finish for interior and exterior woodwork. It will flex with the wood to resist cracking, flaking and peeling. It can be used on new or on previously stained woodwork as well as over sound, previously varnished interior wood.

Brushwood from **Dulux** transforms gloss paint to a natural wood effect with no messy stripping. It is for interior and exterior use. The two-part system comprises Brushwood Basecoat and Brushwood Topcoat from **Dulux**.

Dulux Quick Drying Varnish is a low-odour, solvent-free varnish that is ideal for interior wooden surfaces such as floors and panelling. It is touch dry in 30 minutes and another coat can be added in two hours. It is available in clear gloss, satin and matt finishes.

Dulux Advice Line: For information on any Dulux products or for details of your local stockists, contact: **The Dulux Advice Centre, Wexham Road, Slough SL2 5DS** or call 01753 550555.

Dulux Colour Advice Line: For advice on colour scheming, contact: **The Advice Line** on 0891 51522 (calls cost 49p per minute).